KITTENS

DK PUBLISHING

DK

A DK PUBLISHING BOOK

Writer and editor Carey Scott
US editor Camela Decaire
Designer Sally Geeve
DTP designer Nicky Studdart
Managing editor Linda Martin
Managing art editor Julia Harris
Production Ben Smith

First American edition 1997
2 4 6 8 10 9 7 5 3 1
Published in the United States by DK Publishing, Inc.,
95 Madison Avenue, New York, New York 10016

Published in Great Britain by Dorling Kindersley Ltd.

A catalog record for this book is
available from the Library of Congress.

ISBN 0-7894-2132-1

Color reproduction by G.R.B., Italy
Printed in Italy by L.E.G.O.

CONTENTS

NEWBORN KITTENS

For two weeks after birth, kittens are completely dependent on their mother and will stay close to her, feeding and sleeping. This period of vulnerability is called the neonatal phase. At about ten days old, the kittens' eyes will open, and soon after that their ear flaps will begin to unfold, enabling them to hear clearly. Now kittens enter the socialization phase, when they become more receptive to their surroundings. It is important that they are allowed to stay with their mother until they are fully developed, which takes at least six weeks.

ONE WEEK OLD
A one-week-old kitten is just 6 in (15 cm) long. It should be starting to crawl short distances.

SLEEP HEAP
These little kittens are just a few days old. When their mother is away from them they drag themselves into a "sleep heap" and stay cuddled up together for warmth since they lose heat quickly. Although they cannot see or hear yet, they already have a good sense of smell, which they use to find their mother's nipples.

Eyes are still firmly shut.

Kitten is becoming curious about the world for the first time.

TEN WEEKS OLD
This kitten is now a juvenile, and is well on the way to becoming an adult cat.

FOUR WEEKS OLD
At just four weeks old, kittens leave their mother to explore on their own. It is important that they start getting used to human contact at this age, so it is a good idea to handle your kitten gently for at least one hour a day.

Even though just a few days old, this kitten's coat is particularly luxurious.

CLASSIC LONGHAIRS

It is not only a long coat that distinguishes longhaired cats from other breeds. There are also physical differences and variations in temperament. The heads of longhaired breeds are round and broad, their ears are small, and they have distinctive round eyes. Also, their abundant coats can make them look larger than they really are. In character, longhaired cats tend to be more relaxed and gentle than those with short hair.

DISTINGUISHING MARKS

This breed was originally developed with the intention of imitating the precise markings of a Dutch rabbit. This proved to be almost impossible, but these cats do retain some similar markings, such as an inverted "V" on the face.

Body is stocky and compact, with evenly distributed colored patches.

Black-and-White Bicolor Longhair

**Classic Brown
Tabby Longhairs**

STYLISH RELATIVE
These elegant kittens are cousins
of the common Tabby Shorthairs.
Although they are still very rare,
Tabby Longhairs have been
known in Europe since the end of
the 17th century. They are
characterized by black-based
coats with tawny markings and
orange- or copper-colored eyes.

Reddish-
brown,
symmetrical
markings

RED-HAIRED BEAUTY
This burnt-orange cat has
been a showstopper since
it was first shown in the
United Kingdom in 1895.
In spite of its fiery looks,
this breed has a docile,
friendly temperament.

**Red Persian
Longhair**

Fluffy coat
will become
longer and
silkier as
kitten matures.

PERSIAN LONGHAIRS

Longhaired cats originally came from countries with cold climates, but they are now bred all over the world. These glamorous cats have been bred for their lush, silky fur and unusual markings. Like other longhaired cats, they have a gentle disposition, and require regular brushing if their coats are to stay in tip-top condition.

WORTH HER WEIGHT IN SILVER
This unusual silver-tipped kitten is a variation of the Chinchilla breed, first exhibited at London's Crystal Palace in 1894.

Shaded Silver Longhair

Like Siamese cats, Colorpoints have piercing blue eyes.

PERSIAN AND SIAMESE
These dazzling kittens enjoy the best of both worlds, for they combine the luxurious long hair of the Persian family with the markings and dignity of the Siamese breed.

Seal-point Colorpoint Longhair

Eyes are orange or
copper colored.

Lilac Longhair

Tail is fairly short
and covered with
thick, bushy fur.

The points (feet,
tail, ears, and face)
of a Colorpoint are
a darker color than
the rest of the
body.

NEW BREED

This kitten is an example of a recent
breeding program to develop chocolate
and lilac self-colored longhaired cats, and
is a rare animal. This one has a warm
pinkish-gray coat and a paler ruff, or
"frill." Like Colorpoints, these cats have
some Siamese ancestry and are more
outgoing than Persian cats.

SELF-COLORED KITTENS

Many wild cats have tabby-patterned coats, which provide them with effective camouflage against predators. However, domesticated cats are not hunted by other animals, so protective coloring is not important. Coats of many different colors have evolved, both naturally and through selective breeding. These kittens all have self-colored, or "non-agouti," coats, which means their fur is one color from the tips to the roots.

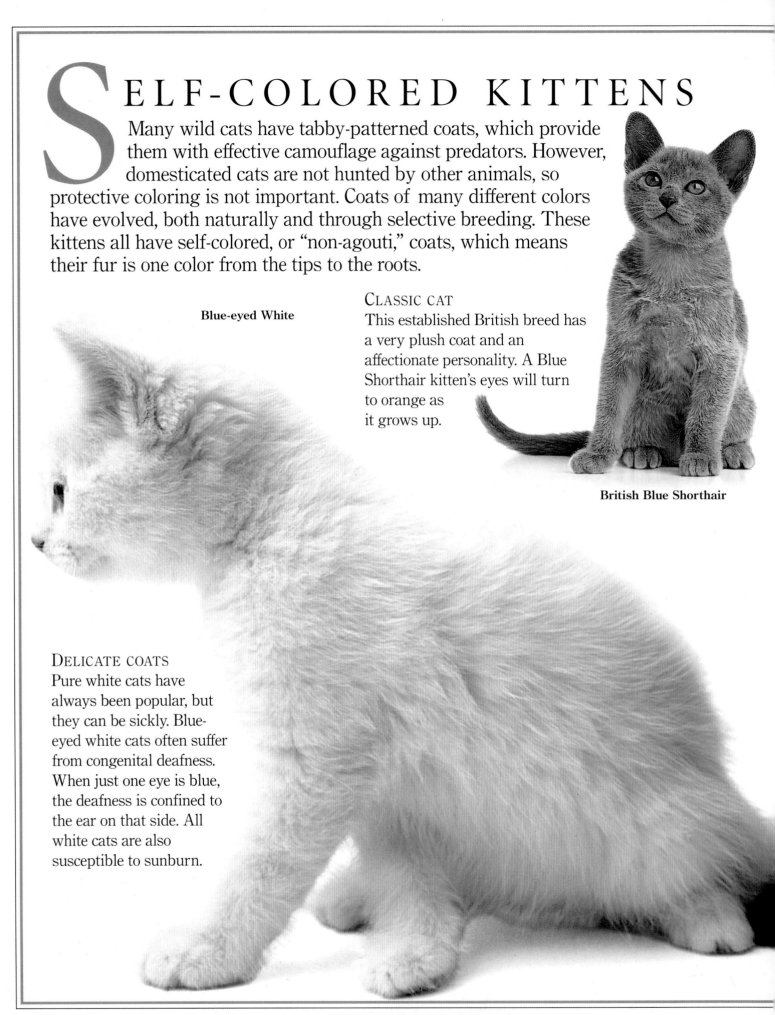

Blue-eyed White

CLASSIC CAT
This established British breed has a very plush coat and an affectionate personality. A Blue Shorthair kitten's eyes will turn to orange as it grows up.

British Blue Shorthair

DELICATE COATS
Pure white cats have always been popular, but they can be sickly. Blue-eyed white cats often suffer from congenital deafness. When just one eye is blue, the deafness is confined to the ear on that side. All white cats are also susceptible to sunburn.

Chocolate and Lilac Shorthairs

NEW COLORS
These unusually colored kittens are recent additions to the British Shorthair breed. Tabby markings are evident in the Lilac kitten, but these should soon disappear, leaving an even, pinkish-gray color.

Fur should be jet-black to the roots.

Nonpedigree Black

"Cobby," or stocky body shape typical of British Shorthair varieties

LUCKY OR NOT
Between the late 1400s and the 17th century, black cats were associated with witchcraft throughout Europe. Large numbers were actually executed because it was believed that they were agents of the devil. However, black cats are now considered to be lucky in many countries.

MARMALADE KITTENS

Ginger, or marmalade, kittens have been known in the United Kingdom since medieval times. After black, an orange coat is probably the oldest color variation. These cats are most numerous in the Far East, Turkey, and North Africa, but can also be found in the western islands of Scotland, where they may have arrived with the Vikings.

NEW BREED
This self-colored kitten from Asia belongs to a new breed. Similar in type to the Burmese, it has a powerful, muscular body and large, oval paws.

Red Cornelian

RED-HOT KITTENS
These Siamese kittens have only pale pink "points" now, but these will become a deeper red as they grow up. They may well develop fiery personalities, too. Siamese cats are natural extroverts and their unusually loud meow is difficult to ignore.

Red-point Siamese

The points (paws, tail, ears, and face) are darker than the rest of the body.

Round-tipped,
medium-sized ears

CLASSIC GINGER

This marmalade kitten may look
like a typical ginger tom at first
glance, but his distinctive
markings and rich red coat
identify him as a pedigree.
British Tabby Shorthairs come in
three patterns: classic, spotted,
and mackerel, and they can be
brown, red, blue, or silver. Whatever
the color, the markings are always a
darker shade than the
background color. In the Classic
Tabby, the markings are
clearly defined and perfectly
symmetrical.

Short,
plush coat

Legs ringed
with "bracelets"
of color

British Red Tabby Shorthair

TABBY KITTENS

All cats are the descendants of the African Wild Cat, and the one that resembles it most closely is the Tabby. The dark, stippled coat, called mackerel because its patterning is similar to that of the fish, provided excellent camouflage for wild cats. However, in the domestic environment, breeding with non-Tabby cats has made this original patterning quite rare. Most modern Tabbies have some blotching on their coats.

Silver Tabby Longhair

ECCENTRIC ANIMALS

Tabby Longhairs first appeared in Europe as long ago as the 17th century, but are much rarer than their shorthaired cousins. This particularly intelligent breed has some decidedly uncatlike habits. Tabby Longhairs sometimes pick up food with their front paws, and they are fond of playing with dripping water!

Traces of ginger are clearly evident in the coat.

CATNAPPING

More cats are seen with tabby markings than any other type of coat because the tabby gene is dominant. When cats breed naturally, variations in the markings and color are left to nature. These young kittens enjoy naps, cuddled up together in a confined space. Even when your kitten is fully grown, it will still like the security and comfort of sleeping in a small space, like a shoebox.

Tabby Maine Coon

Thick coat evolved in response to the harsh Maine winters.

Blue Spotted Tabby Shorthair

HARDY BREED

This cat belongs to one of the oldest and largest American breeds. It is descended from farm cats in the state of Maine, where its ancestors prospered on a diet of rabbits. Today these cats make companionable pets.

DISTINCTIVELY SPOTTED

Spotted cats were common in ancient Egypt and the pattern still occurs in a number of breeds today. Spotted Tabbies, or Ticked Tabbies, as they are known in the US, have dense, short fur covered in numerous spots.

Closed eyes and contented expression show kitten is secure and cozy.

Nonpedigree Tabby-and-White Shorthairs

Tabby markings are most prominent on the back.

TORTOISESHELL KITTENS

In the wild camouflage is important for animals hiding from predators – particularly so for female cats with young kittens. Tortoiseshell cats' dark, mottled coloring makes them almost imperceptible against a variety of backgrounds. It is no coincidence that the tortoiseshell gene is sex linked, occurring almost exclusively in female cats. Although familiar, Tortoiseshell cats are hard to breed. Females are best mated with a solid-colored black, red, or cream male, but the litter may contain only one or two Tortoiseshell kittens.

NEW BLUE BREED
All types of Tortoiseshells are known for their gentle and affectionate natures, including this new breed. She has blue and cream in her coat instead of the usual red and black.

CLASSIC CAT
This alert, playful kitten has the characteristic tortoiseshell coat of black, red, and cream patches. Very occasionally, male cats are born with this coloring, but they are usually sterile.

Blue Tortoiseshell-and-White Shorthair

Tortoiseshell Shorthair

Tortoishell-and-White Shorthair

CALICO CAT
If this kitten inherits the characteristics of her breed, she will grow up to be a devoted mother and a champion mouser. In the US she is called a Calico because her color-splashed coat resembles the printed cotton.

MANY-COLORED CAT
This breed, defined by patches of white, black, and red in varying shades, used to be known as the Chintz or Spanish Cat.

Tortoiseshell-and-White Longhair

Solid body and dense, silky coat

ORIENTAL BREEDS

In place of the stocky, or "cobby," build of the typical European cat, those from the Far East have slender, muscular bodies and long, narrow faces rather than round. In temperament they can be described as energetic, affectionate, and unusually intelligent – or as attention-seeking, noisy, and highly strung. Both descriptions are accurate – depending on personal taste!

Tonkinese

SOFT AS MINK

These kittens are the result of a cross between a Siamese and a Burmese cat. They are bred in various shades and are called Minks because of their unusually soft fur.

Slightly slanted, sapphire-blue eyes

Birmans

EXOTIC HISTORY

Birman cats are said to be descended from cats that once guarded a sacred temple in Burma. They first came to Europe in 1919, when two Birman cats were given to Major Gordon Russell in France by priests he had helped escape from Tibet.

BEGUILING CREATURES

Several breeds of cats developed in Siam (now Thailand), but the Siamese is the most popular because it was a favorite of Thai royalty. This is the most exaggerated of Oriental breeds and the most extrovert of all domestic cats. It has a lithe, athletic body, a short-furred coat, large, pointed ears, and vivid blue eyes. Siamese cats are usually devoted to their owners, and may even become jealous of rivals to their master's affections.

Siamese

Semi-longhaired coat does not matt and only requires light brushing.

REGAL BREEDS

Cats were first domesticated in the Middle East about 4,000 years ago. In Turkey, white Angoras were kept as pets in Constantinople (now Istanbul) harems, while in ancient Egypt, cats were worshiped. During the cult of the fertility goddess Bastet, which lasted for nearly 2,000 years, cats were believed to be the embodiment of the goddess herself. They were so revered that it was a capital offense to kill a cat, and when one died, the whole household went into mourning.

ELEGANT ABYSSINIAN
This breed was first brought to Europe in 1868 by soldiers returning from war in Abyssinia (now Ethiopia). It is said to be a direct descendant of ancient Egyptian cats, although some breeders dispute this.

Abyssinian

Coat color is called Sorrel, and is one of a number of varieties.

Cinnamon Angora

NOBLE GIFTS
These wide-eyed kittens belong to one of the oldest longhaired breeds, which originated in Ankara in Turkey. In the 16th century, Angoras were presented as gifts to European nobles by Turkish sultans. This attractive cinnamon variety looks more oriental than the original Turkish breed.

Long, fine, silky coat

Characteristic "M" marking on forehead

Egyptian Mau

MEOW MAU
Mau is the ancient Egyptian word meaning "sacred domestic cat." It is believed to be a natural breed from the Cairo area of Egypt, and its markings are remarkably similar to those depicted on ancient Egyptian scrolls and tomb paintings.

CURIOUS KITTENS

It was at the beginning of the 20th century that people started to breed cats selectively. It was soon discovered that almost any feline feature could be adapted – cats could have longer fur, shorter tails, or larger ears – although many people think this practice is cruel. These mutations might appear naturally from time to time, but would probably not be passed on.

Sphynx

COATLESS CAT
The almost hairless Sphynx was bred from a kitten born in Ontario, Canada, in 1966. The lack of a furry coat makes these cats vulnerable to both cold and heat.

Manx

TALE OF TAILS
Cats without tails first appeared on the Isle of Man, off the west coast of England, at least 200 years ago. According to legend, the first Manx cat lost its tail when Noah closed the door to the Ark a bit too quickly! Whatever their origin, Manx cats have developed powerful bodies and do not seem to suffer at all from the lack of a tail.

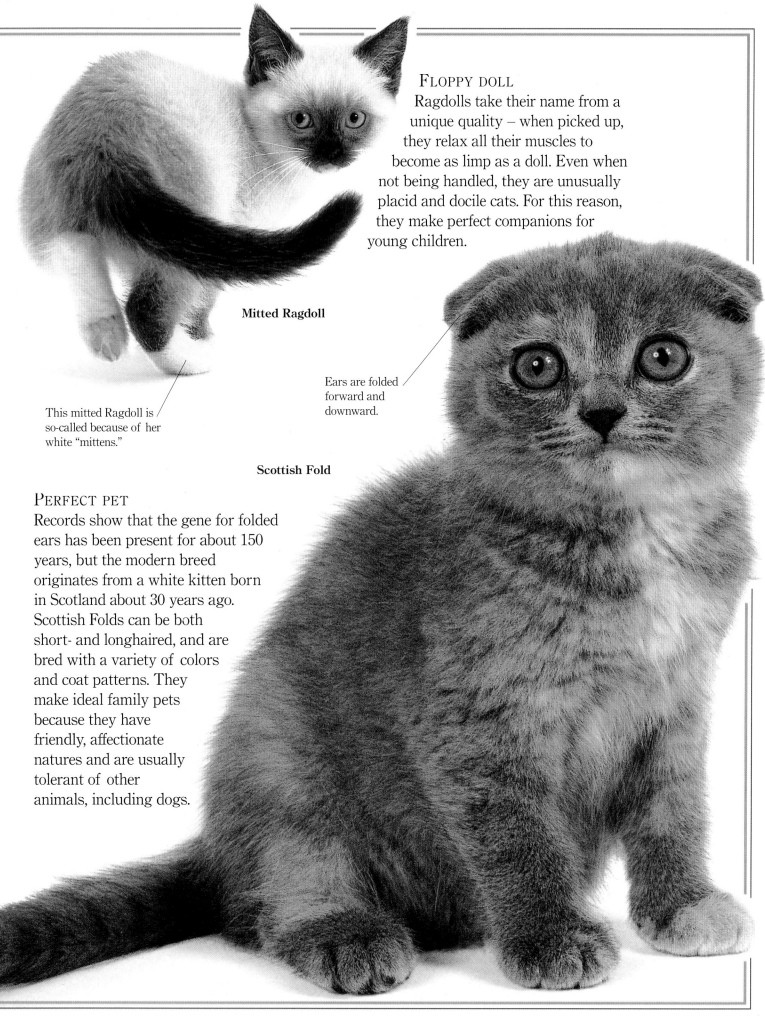

FLOPPY DOLL

Ragdolls take their name from a unique quality – when picked up, they relax all their muscles to become as limp as a doll. Even when not being handled, they are unusually placid and docile cats. For this reason, they make perfect companions for young children.

Mitted Ragdoll

This mitted Ragdoll is so-called because of her white "mittens."

Ears are folded forward and downward.

Scottish Fold

PERFECT PET

Records show that the gene for folded ears has been present for about 150 years, but the modern breed originates from a white kitten born in Scotland about 30 years ago. Scottish Folds can be both short- and longhaired, and are bred with a variety of colors and coat patterns. They make ideal family pets because they have friendly, affectionate natures and are usually tolerant of other animals, including dogs.

NONPEDIGREE KITTENS

Nonpedigree cats are probably the most common in the world. They are usually shorthairs, with stocky builds and round faces, and are found in a full range of colors. Nonpedigrees can be both mongrels and crossbreeds; a crossbreed is the result of parents of different pedigrees, while a mongrel comes from nonpedigree parentage.

White-and-Tortoiseshell

TWO CAN BE BETTER THAN ONE
Like any two kittens, these nonpedigrees are capable of becoming close companions if they grow up together. A single cat can be lonely, so if you spend a lot of time away from home you should consider having two.

White facial blaze

Different-colored coats is one sign of more than one father.

MIXED LITTER

When a female cat is in heat, she may mate with several males. This can result in there being more than one father of the kittens in a litter, and is the reason kittens from the same litter can look very different from one another.

Cat will rub its face against bark to spread its scent.

Getting up is easy, but climbing down is more difficult, especially for kittens.

Tail is used as a counterweight to provide balance.

Tabby-and-White Shorthairs

BALANCED MOVEMENT

Even though cats have the best-developed sense of balance of all mammals, they do sometimes lose their footing. All cats, however, can correct their body position while falling to make sure they land safely. Cats can also judge distances and spaces accurately. Both the whiskers and the guard (outer) hairs are extremely sensitive to the tiniest pressure.

CHOOSING YOUR KITTEN

Deciding on the right type of kitten can be difficult. You may be attracted to a certain type of cat because of its looks, but remember that longhaired cats need regular grooming, and Oriental cats can be demanding. If it is a companion you want rather than a showpiece, a nonpedigree may be the best bet for you. There are no serious breed weaknesses in cats, and pedigree and nonpedigree cats have similar lifespans.

Gums and tongue should be pink and clean.

Eyes should be clear, bright, and free from any discharge.

Check for flea infestation, which can be detected quite easily by any specks of dried blood in the fur.

Kitten should be alert and interested in its surroundings.

STEPS TO HEALTH AND HAPPINESS

There are certain steps you can take to guarantee that your kitten is in good health and will grow up to be a well-adjusted cat. First, never buy a kitten younger than eight weeks old. Second, do not buy from a pet store where animals may be maltreated. Instead, go to friends or neighbors, or a recommended breeder if you are buying a pedigree. Always inspect the kitten of your choice thoroughly to make sure it is free from disease or infection.

Coat should be sleek and glossy.

CARING FOR KITTENS

Protein, in the form of canned cat food, fresh meat, or fish, should form 35–40 percent of a kitten's, and 25 percent of an adult cat's, diet. The remainder should ideally be made up of different foods. A varied diet means a balanced diet, and will prevent your kitten from becoming a fussy eater. After eating, a kitten will usually wash itself thoroughly. A cat is a very clean animal and possesses the perfect grooming tool – a rough tongue. However, regular combing or brushing will guarantee a perfect coat.

A kitten's sensitive sense of smell enables it to tell if food is fresh. It will not eat fish or meat that is rotten.

LIQUID ASSETS
Most cats like milk, but it can give them an upset stomach, so water should always be available. However, don't worry if your cat does not drink very much. Cats do not need a lot of liquid as their kidneys are very efficient at conserving water. Nevertheless, it is important that your kitten always has access to fresh, clean water.

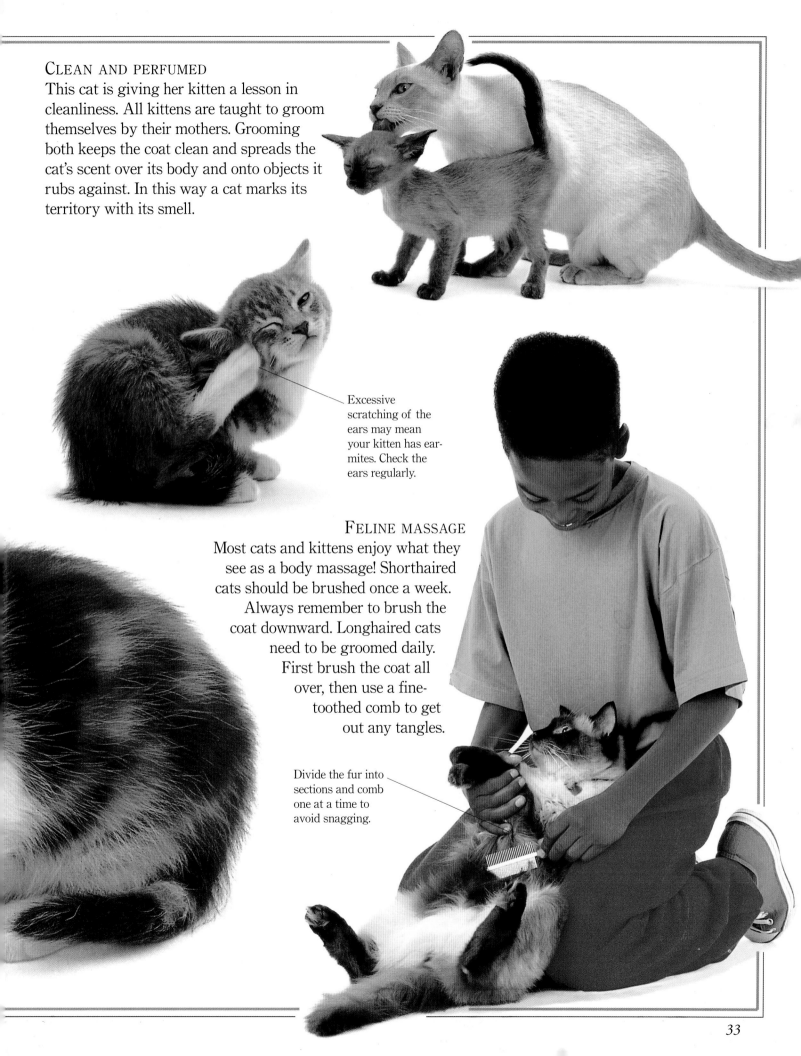

CLEAN AND PERFUMED

This cat is giving her kitten a lesson in cleanliness. All kittens are taught to groom themselves by their mothers. Grooming both keeps the coat clean and spreads the cat's scent over its body and onto objects it rubs against. In this way a cat marks its territory with its smell.

Excessive scratching of the ears may mean your kitten has ear-mites. Check the ears regularly.

FELINE MASSAGE

Most cats and kittens enjoy what they see as a body massage! Shorthaired cats should be brushed once a week. Always remember to brush the coat downward. Longhaired cats need to be groomed daily. First brush the coat all over, then use a fine-toothed comb to get out any tangles.

Divide the fur into sections and comb one at a time to avoid snagging.

KITTEN COMFORTS

Your kitten will probably be confused and nervous when it first arrives in its new home. Help it settle in by making a fuss over it and playing with it. All kittens enjoy playing. It helps them develop quick reactions, exercises their limbs, and provides hours of entertainment. But all that running around can be exhausting, and kittens love to sleep as much as they love to play. On average, cats spend 16 hours of every day asleep. They do not sleep in long stretches like us, but "catnap" in a series of short sleeps.

Mouse for chasing

Catnip

Feather

TOYS FOR KITTENS
You can buy special toys from pet stores, but your kitten will be just as happy with homemade toys, like old thread spools and scrunched-up paper.

SPORTING HUNTERS
Like their wild cousins, domestic cats play with their prey before killing it. In fact, they are much more interested in hunting for sport than for a square meal. Kittens, and some adult cats, will enjoy practicing their hunting skills on a toy bird or mouse, or even a ball of yarn!

Fixed look indicates high level of concentration.

A specially provided basket should mean you won't have to share your bed with your kitten.

SNUGNESS

Every kitten and cat likes to sleep somewhere that smells of its owner. This is probably why they often take over the bed or favorite armchair. Line a basket with an old item of clothing, and the reassuring smell will encourage your kitten to make this its permanent sleeping place.

Clean the box thoroughly once a week and remove used litter daily.

TOILET TRAINING

Introduce the litter box when your kitten starts on solid food, which should be at around four weeks. Place it in a quiet spot and put your kitten on it when you see her crouching with her tail raised. Cats are naturally clean animals and usually learn to use their litter boxes very quickly.

USEFUL ADDRESSES

American Cat Association
8101 Katherine Avenue
Panorama City, CA 91402
Ph: (818) 781-5656

American Society for the Prevention of Cruelty to Animals
424 East 92nd Street
New York, NY 10128
Ph: (212) 876-7700

The Cat Fanciers Association
Po Box 1005
Manasquan, NJ 08736-1005
Ph: (908) 528-9797

Humane Society of the United States
2100 L Street
NW Washington, DC 20037
Ph: (202) 452-1100

The International Cat Association
PO Box 2684
Harlingen, TX 78551
Ph: (210) 428-8046

Best Friends Animal Sanctuary
PO Box G
Kanab, UT 84741-5001
Ph: (801) 644-2001

PHOTOGRAPHIC CREDITS

The publisher would like to thank the following for their kind permission to reproduce their photographs:

KEY: *t* top; *c* center; *b* bottom; *l* left; *r* right

Pat Doyle: 14-15*b*

Tetsu Yamazaki: 26*tr*

Photographers:

Paul Bricknell: 24*b*, 28, 33*b*, 37*b*

Jane Burton: *End papers*, 5, 6*tl, tr, bl, br*, 7*tl, tr, br*, 8-9, 22*t*, 23*t*, 18-19*b*, 27*t*, 29*t, r*, 30-31, 32*b*, 33*t*, c, 36*tl, tr*, 37*tl, tr,*

Steven Gorton and **Tim Ridley**: 14*t*, 32*t*

Marc Henrie: 7*bl*, 11*t*, 12*tl*, 13*tr*, 15*t*, 16*t*, 25*t, b*, 18*t*, 19*tl, tr*, 27*b*

Dave King: 10, 11*b*, 16*b*, 17, 22-23*b*, 26*b*, 36*b*

Steve Shott: 12-13*b*

INDEX